Giving Feedback

Pocket Mentor Series

The books in this series offer immediate solutions to the challenges managers face every day. Each book is packed with handy tools, checklists, and real-life examples, including a Test Yourself section to help identify strengths and weaknesses. For all readers eager to address the daily demands of work, these books are ideal.

Books in the series:
Leading Teams
Running Meetings
Managing Time
Managing Projects
Coaching People
Giving Feedback
Leading People

Giving
Feedback

Expert Solutions to Everyday Challenges

Harvard Business School Press

Boston, Massachusetts

No part of this publication may be reproduced, stored in or introduced into a re-
trieval system, or transmitted, in any form, or by any means (electronic, mechanical,
photocopying, recording, or otherwise), without the prior permission of the pub-
lisher. Requests for permission should be directed to permissions@hbsp.harvard.edu,
or mailed to Permissions, Harvard Business School Publishing, 60 Harvard Way,
Boston, Massachusetts 02163.

Library of Congress Cataloging-in-Publication Data
Pocket mentor. Giving feedback : expert solutions to everyday challenges.
    p. cm. — (Pocket mentor series)
   Includes bibliographical references.
   ISBN-13: 978-1-4221-0348-7 (pbk. : alk. paper)
   ISBN-10: 1-4221-0348-X
   1. Communication in personnel management. 2. Communication in
management. 3. Interpersonal communication. 4. Feedback (Psychology)
I. Harvard Business School Publishing Corporation.
  HF5549.5.C6G58 2006
  658.4'5—dc22

                             2006034447

The paper used in this publication meets the requirements of the American National
Standard for Permanence of Paper for Publications and Documents in Libraries and
Archives Z39.48-1992

Contents

To Learn More   67

Additional titles of articles and books if you want to go more deeply into the topic.

Sources for Giving Feedback   75

Notes   77

For you to use as ideas come to mind.

Mentor's Message: Feedback as a path for learning, developing, and changing

Feedback is, first and foremost, about learning, developing, and changing. The organizations we manage, the people we work with and supervise, and we ourselves as managers all have to learn, develop, and change in order to survive, let alone prosper, in today's increasingly complex and rapidly evolving business world. Indeed, the need for feedback, both at the organizational and individual level, underlies virtually all management, leadership development, and organizational change challenges we face. Given these realities, building our skill at giving feedback and opening ourselves to receiving feedback from others remain critical success factors for effective management today.

Yet all too often feedback is perceived as difficult, and it is avoided or postponed until the opportunity to give feedback is lost in the fast shuffle of other events. When this happens, not only do the individuals involved lose a learning opportunity, but our organizations suffer from that lost learning when unproductive patterns of behavior continue or successful behavior is not reinforced and celebrated.

As with many of the challenges of interpersonal relationships, the difficulties of giving and receiving feedback usually stem from lack of knowledge, skill, and practice. The following guide provides a wealth of practical ideas and tools to help you get better at giving and receiving feedback so that the learning from feedback can be heard and used. The challenge for you is to take what is offered here and practice it. Learn from the successes and the failures as you practice your feedback skills—you can even work on getting feedback on how you provide feedback!

As a consultant to many organizations facing various challenges, I have found a few important consistencies throughout organizational life, regardless of the nature of the business. One of them is that organizational systems characterized by frequent and open feedback, with a balance of both "positive" and "constructive" messages, tend to have employees who feel committed, valued, and willing to learn and change. Organizations where feedback is lacking, or where it is disproportionately limited to critical performance management conversations, tend to have employees who are suspicious; withholding of their commitment, ideas, and energy; and cynical about management. You can choose the impact you have on your organizational culture in part by how well and consistently you choose to learn and practice the tools of feedback.

I hope this guide will be useful to you in your own personal learning, development, and growth as a manager.

Jamie O. Harris, Mentor
Interaction Associates, Inc.

Jamie O. Harris is a Senior Associate with Interaction Associates, Inc., where he provides organizational change consulting services to both public and private sector clients and leads workshops on facilitation skills, leadership, and collaborative change. He also serves as the company's corporate counsel, having practiced business and real estate law for more than 20 years before joining Interaction Associates. Mr. Harris received his BA in political science and economics and his JD from Yale University.

Giving Feedback: The Basics

What Is Feedback?

It takes two to speak the truth—one to speak and one to hear.
—Henry David Thoreau

Feedback is supposed to be a healthy tonic for workplace productivity, and yet many people are anxious about the moment of feedback. Feedback is just *not* considered "fun"!

Why?

For many people, the word *feedback* seems to mean *judgment*, so that neither giver nor receiver looks forward to those feedback moments. The receiver often creates a shield to block the expected negative message. The giver wants to avoid sounding too much like a scolding parent and damaging a sound working relationship.

But feedback shouldn't be a judgment about another person's character. Rather, feedback is meant to be an objective message about behavior and consequences, either as recognition of a job well done or a suggestion on how to improve on the job. The goal of feedback is to encourage the recipient of the feedback to move forward by learning, growing, and changing.

Feedback *n* **1:** the flow of information among associates, usually as an evaluation of a project or work completed **2:** the sharing of observations about job performance or work-related behaviors **3:** the first step toward positive, productive change

---

What feedback is *not*!

Feedback is *not* a form of punishment. After all, the act of feeding provides nourishment; it enables another person to grow in a healthy manner. So keep in mind that:

- Feedback is *not* necessarily negative.

- Feedback is *not* a one-way monologue.

- Feedback does *not* need to be a wrestling match.

- Feedback is *not* an opportunity for a personal attack.

- Feedback does *not* represent the *only* point of view.

Tip: If you want to improve continuously as a manager, then you have to have feedback—and you have to know how to give it as well as receive it.

What feedback *is*

Giving and receiving feedback in a professional setting is a critical part of managing people, interacting with colleagues, and listening to your associates at work. Feedback comes from clients and customers as well. It is feedback—or other people's responses to behaviors, processes, or results—that fosters positive change and increases self-awareness.

The goal of giving positive feedback is to reinforce preferred behaviors or patterns of problem solving. For corrective feedback, on the other hand, the goal is to change and improve unsatisfactory behavior or introduce more productive work patterns so that the recipient learns new ways to behave or respond to changes.

You can give feedback in different directions: up to those to whom you report, down to those you manage, and laterally to your colleagues.

Or, you may *receive* feedback from any of these directions as well. Viewed from this multidirectional perspective, feedback is an important contributor to organizational learning.

After a new production run has been tested, your direct report shows you an innovative way to reduce the run time by easing a bottleneck that has been slowing down the process.

Note that this feedback is directed at improving the work process by helping you learn a new method of solving a particular type of problems. It is not a personal criticism but a specific suggestion for productive change.

Why is feedback important?

Giving and receiving feedback is valuable for many reasons. When you give constructive feedback to others, you are

- reinforcing or encouraging an effective way of working

- redirecting a behavior or pointing out a more productive path of action

- preparing for better performance
- contributing to learning and developing for the recipient

When others give honest feedback to you, you can improve

- your relationships with them by showing how well you interact with people
- your work process by the way you get the work done
- your results by measurable on-the-job achievements
- your awareness of the impact of your own behavior and actions on others

"In my experience, employee development depends on feedback; it provides the guideposts for growth, motivation, and, ultimately, morale. Without constructive one-on-one communication and feedback, many employees are left feeling ineffectual, frustrated, or disaffected."
—Peter Baskette, manager

Feedback is a basic skill managers develop in order to work with others. This skill comes into play not only during the day-to-day work that must get done, but also during coaching sessions, delegating tasks, and formal performance assessments.

"Nothing good ever happens when feedback is lacking."
—Steve Armstrong, vice president, Kelly Services

Feedback? Coaching? Performance evaluations? What's the difference?

	FEEDBACK	COACHING	PERFORMANCE EVALUATION
Purpose	To reinforce or change behavior	To improve skills	To evaluate past work
Participants	Any two (or more) people	Typically supervisor to direct report, but can be multidirectional	Supervisor to direct report
Place	Private and quiet space	Depends on the skill to be learned	Usually in the supervisor's office
Tone	Typically casual, although can be more formal	Somewhat formal, but potentially relaxed	Very formal; often stressful
Timing	Impromptu as needed or during formal sessions	Regular meetings	Scheduled every six months or once a year
Follow-up	Continual	Continual	Based on action plan

When to Give Feedback

People tend to give feedback right away, in an impromptu manner. This immediate response can be very useful because the incident is fresh in everyone's minds. However, there is the danger of reacting too quickly to a situation, before you have the necessary facts and information or while people's feelings may still be too turbulent or brittle.

Know when to step in

In some ways, knowing when to give feedback is easier than you may realize; you just have to train yourself to recognize those appropriate moments when they occur. Offer feedback when these types of situations arise:

- When good work, successful projects, and resourceful behavior need to be recognized. Positive feedback is not given often enough and yet its benefits can be great.

- When the probability of successfully improving a person's skills is high. Skills that can be learned are more easily changed than a person's habits or personality.

- When a problem cannot be ignored; when the person's behavior has a negative impact on the team or organization.

You can be flexible and sensitive to the situation when deciding to give feedback:

- You may decide to provide feedback as soon as you can after you observe the behavior you want to correct or reinforce.

- You may need to pause long enough to gather all the necessary information before discussing an issue with the recipient.

- If the behavior you observed was particularly upsetting, you may need to give everyone time to calm down.

The right time depends on the situation and on the recipient. Try to determine whether the person is ready to accept your message; otherwise, the feedback might not really be heard.

Tip: Give positive feedback often. Affirming the high quality of your direct report's work is one of the most effective ways of retaining that valuable employee.

When feedback works and when it doesn't

Feedback is more likely to affect learning, growth, and change in areas that least threaten the recipient's sense of self-worth. The table below indicates that learning new job skills is usually the easiest type

HELPING PEOPLE CHANGE: EASY TO DIFFICULT

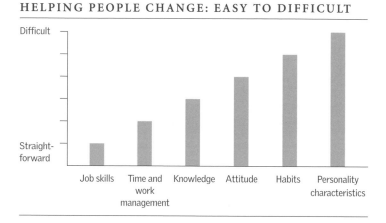

of change a person can make, whereas altering inherent personality characteristics is the most difficult.

Given these general tendencies, try to use feedback to enhance and improve a person's

- job skills (for example, learning a new computer program)
- time management skills (for example, prioritizing tasks)
- work process (for example, establishing a logical routine)
- knowledge about a subject or organization (for example, learning new tax codes)

Tip: Never schedule a feedback session for a Friday afternoon.

On the other hand, avoid giving feedback when a change is too difficult for the person or beyond a person's control.

A manager asks an introverted direct report to become more of a people person instead of addressing the person's specific job behaviors that could be changed.

Changing a person's attitudes or habits is possible but takes more of a commitment than the typical feedback process. Feedback directed to this kind of change will need to be sustained over time and focused on long-term learning, not just immediate results. Long-term learning typically becomes a coaching situation rather than feedback.

How to Give Feedback Effectively

Give the employee
a goal to work for, not a legacy to overcome.
—Hal Plotkin

In general, when giving feedback, concentrate on improving performance—don't use feedback simply to criticize by stating your preconceived judgment. Make sure the feedback is future-focused; pick issues that can be reworked in the future. For example, if a behavior or action was a one-time event, you might let it go.

Establish a receptive work environment

As a manager, you establish the tone, the feel, and even the culture for working in your group. Take advantage of this prerogative to adopt a broad and general acceptance that feedback is a mutually beneficial exchange.

You can achieve this attitude of mutual benefit toward feedback by

- basing feedback on clear work expectations

- establishing a mutual commitment between individuals or groups to work on areas that need improvement

- acknowledging positive performance

- framing feedback as an ongoing process—not as an occasional or arbitrary comment or correction

---

Tip: For feedback to be accepted, the receiver has to view the giver as reliable and as having good intentions.

Do your homework before a formal feedback session

Most feedback may be on-the-go responses to immediate situations; however, formal feedback sessions can also provide a more orderly process for learning and growth. To prepare for a formal feedback session:

- Gather all the data, facts, and information you need to present an objective view of the issue.

- Consider the recipient's point of view. Try to understand who she is and how she wants to grow.

- Anticipate her response to the feedback session.

- Adapt your communication style to hers, if possible. (For example, if she's an outgoing, social kind of person, start with an upbeat note about her work.)

- Be sensitive to ways in which gender, race, age, or other differences might affect her response to your feedback.

What Would YOU Do?

Every Time We Say Goodbye

RON COULD NOT HELP but notice that Katy almost slammed the door on her way out. Actually, he had to admit that she did slam it. Why was she mad at him again? Every time he tried to help her improve her skills, she became very sensitive. This time he had pointed out—in a polite, objective fashion—that the way she kept her desk was causing her to work less efficiently. Sometimes she misplaced things, and wasted time rummaging around trying to find them. What was the big deal? You'd think he'd told her she was about to lose her job, which was ridiculous. Katy was a productive employee who had good people skills, really creative ideas, and plenty of follow-through. Naturally, since she was already doing the big things right, there was no need to waste both of their time discussing them. Focus on areas that need improvement—that was Ron's approach. Why didn't it seem to work with Katy?

"Organizational systems characterized by frequent and open feedback, with a balance of both 'positive' and 'constructive' messages, tend to have employees who feel committed, valued, and willing to learn and change."

—Jamie Harris, mentor

Planning a Feedback Session

Use this tool to organize before giving feedback during a scheduled session.

Name the issue or behavior that needs to be corrected or reinforced.

A helpdesk provider was rude to a customer during a customer service call.

What is the impact of the issue or behavior on the team, in the department, or on the project?

The other helpdesk providers overheard the rude comments and were distressed about their teammate's behavior. Such behavior could potentially damage our department's reputation. The customer complained to me as manager that she is dissatisfied with our service.

What details do you have to describe the behavior accurately? (who, what, when)

I need to explain the customer's description of the event and her complaint to Gonzalo. The details seem to be that Gonzalo spoke in a sharp tone of voice and said that he didn't know how long the server would be down. When the customer asked again when service would be restarted, Gonzalo shouted that he couldn't help her.

What is the specific purpose of the feedback?

The purposes of this feedback session are 1) give Gonzalo the facts as I understand them, 2) ask Gonzalo about the events, 3) make it clear that the behavior will not be tolerated, but also 4) see if there are ways to help Gonzalo and the other helpdesk employees avoid such frustrating moments.

Describe possible barriers to giving this feedback. What can you do to overcome them?

Gonzalo may be angry and anxious. He may not want to talk about the event. He may want to defend himself rather than giving me a more unbiased description of the event. I will try not to seem judgmental when Gonzalo arrives. I will give Gonzalo my full attention.

What results do you want to produce? In the short run? In the long term?

I want Gonzalo to understand that he must control his emotions when he talks with customers. I also want to see if there is some way to make Gonzalo's environment less frustrating for him and his team.

Evaluating the Feedback Process

Use this chart after you have given feedback to determine what part of the process, relationship, and results worked and what areas could be changed or improved.

Topic	What worked?	What could be changed or improved?
Process		
Planning for the meeting	• Listening carefully to the customer's account of the episode • Gathering information from records and tapes and from other helpdesk team members	
Setting the beginning of the meeting up for success	• Greeting Gonzalo in a friendly manner • Complimenting him on his work • Describing the problem in detail	
Having a clear and logical process	• Knowing what I will say for the first part of the meeting • Trying to be open for the rest, whichever way it goes	The meeting went well, but if Gonzalo had been angry, I couldn't have handled the meeting as well. I need to prepare more for different scenarios.
Developing a realistic action plan	We agreed on future behavior and plans to help support the helpdesk team.	We still need to sit down and develop a formal action plan.
Relationship		
Communication style	Open, friendly, honest—it's the right way to work with Gonzalo.	
Reaction to the feedback	Gonzalo admitted that he was the one who was rude to the customer. He was apologetic, not angry.	
Level of trust	Gonzalo trusted me to listen to his version of the event and the reasons for his behavior.	

Topic	What worked?	What could be changed or improved?
Relationship		
Level of mutual respect and learning	Because I value him and he trusts me, he could be honest about the reasons for his behavior but still accept responsibility.	
Results		
Impact of changes	All the helpdesk providers, especially Gonzalo, have been extremely polite to customer callers. Callers seem to be pleased with the messages and help they receive.	I am encouraging the team to continue their excellent behavior.
Timeliness of changes	Immediate	Will the team's excellent behavior last?
Expectations met	So far!	I'll keep following up and give the team and individual members positive feedback.

Follow these five steps to facilitate a corrective feedback session

Corrective feedback is more difficult to provide than positive rein-
forcement, but, of course, it's an essential tool for managers to use
to improve individual and organizational productivity.

1. Identify a specific employee behavior. Is the employee sloppy in
his reports? Does he come into work late? Does he talk too loudly
on the telephone? When you meet with him, be as precise as possible. For example, don't say, "Alex, you're late to work all the time."
Do say, "Alex, during the past month, you've come into the office an
hour late eight times."

Choose your words carefully to keep the focus on the other person. For example, say, "I want to make sure you understand." Don't say, "I want to make sure I've made myself clear."

2. Stop talking and start listening. Avoid talking too much; you want to hear the other person's perspective. Once you have described the problem behavior to the employee, encourage self-assessment and pay close attention to how the employee responds—and be sure to both listen to the words and read the body language.

- Listen actively. Concentrate on the employee's message and its implications rather than on your response. In particular, listen to what he is describing, how he feels as shown through body language, and what images and metaphors he uses.

- Paraphrase what the employee says. By restating his response in different words, you will show the employee that you have understood his point. If you haven't understood, ask more questions until both of you are sure you understand.

Tip: Focus on job performance, skills, behavior—things that can be changed most easily.

"Focus on actions rather than on your conclusions."
—Jack H. Grossman and J. Robert Parkinson

Steps to Facilitate Corrective Feedback

1. Identify a specific employee behavior.
2. Stop talking and start listening.
3. Agree on what the issue is.
4. Agree on an action plan.
5. Follow up.

3. Agree on what the issue is. After expressing your concern and listening to his response, identifying the issue may be very easy. But that's not always the case. Sometimes the surface behavior is the result of a deeper problem. If, for example, the employee is late to work, you may both agree that's the issue, but you aren't looking at the underlying causes. He may be late to work because he's having problems at home, or he may be unhappy about work and resisting coming into the office. He may be simply unconcerned about time, but he concentrates on getting his work done.

Step back and look at the larger picture before you move on to developing an action plan. Don't be afraid to be wrong. You may be learning as much as the other person through the give-and-take process.

Tip: During a feedback session, make the person comfortable. Don't meet on opposite sides of a desk, and never answer the phone!

---

4. Agree on an action plan. Once you know what the issues are, you can work together to develop an action plan. The plan has to address the most immediate problem. In this case, the employee is often late to work and his behavior lowers the morale of those employees who do come in on time.

Consider different types of solutions. You could

- Offer the carrot: Find more interesting and satisfying assignments for the employee to work on as an incentive to arrive on time.

- Use the stick: Demand that he be prompt and establish explicit consequences for tardiness (for example, denying an office privilege).

- Seek an alternative: Allow a flexible schedule for the entire group so that everyone would have the option of coming into the office within a range of times.

Tip: Provide the explicit evidence and the reasoning that led you to the conclusion that a problem exists.

Tip: Control your own body language during a feedback session—don't yawn, crack your knuckles, or gaze out the window.

What You COULD Do.

Remember Ron's dilemma?

Here's what the mentor suggests:

Ron might begin first by examining his own motives in dealing with what he perceives to be Katy's "problem." If she is productive, good with people, creative, and follows through well, what really is the issue? Is he reacting more to his own need for order and control or is he responding to a real need for her to change and improve for her own benefit? Does her misplacing things or "wasting time rummaging" have a real impact on others, or is it just something that annoys Ron? By putting her desktop habits in perspective, he might be better able either to ignore them or to frame an approach to feedback—if it is really needed—that would be more successful.

Next, Ron should reevaluate his idea that "there's no need to waste time" on the positives. *Au contraire*! There is probably much to be gained from focusing on the positives with Katy. She is doing the important things right, and Ron's withholding positive feedback while criticizing minor foibles may well be leading Katy to feel that he is nitpicking and critical by nature and that he fails to notice the good things she is doing. No wonder that she might react with frustration. Quality time spent on positive feedback—which seems to be well deserved—with less time focused on the minor corrections he is asking for would probably change how she hears the feedback and how she sees her boss as a supportive person.

5. Follow up. For the sake of the employee, your team, and the organization, don't stop the process of change when the meeting ends. Continue to see how he's doing, whether he's following the agreed-upon action plan. If the problem persists, you may be able to use more informal feedback moments successfully, or you may have to move on to more severe measures.

How to Receive Feedback Openly

Success in the marketplace increasingly depends on learning,
yet most people don't know how to learn.

—Chris Argyris

Positive feedback feels as good as a pat on the back, but corrective feedback can be more difficult to hear, accept, and act upon. Receiving feedback with an open mind is just as important as giving it, even though, on some level, you may feel defensive about suggestions for improving your skills, attitudes, or productivity.

Why do we feel defensive?

Dedicated professionals often tell themselves: "By now I should know it all! After all, I've worked hard, I'm highly skilled, and I'm committed to my work."

Corrective feedback directed at you implies that you've made a mistake, that you've failed in some way. Failure, in itself, is threatening to most professional people who pride themselves on their high-quality work. The internal logic often reasons that the best way to avoid failure is to be perfect all the time. To be perfect, stick with what you already know and do well. So, the logic goes: Avoid learning new skills, ideas, processes, behavior; then, you won't ever fail.

Once your defenses are up, even the best feedback can bounce right off that defensive wall and turn toward blaming another person—an unfair supervisor or a stupid client.

Open your mind to change

The secret to receiving feedback is to open your mind to hear the feedback, to acknowledge that you can learn from mistakes or even failures, and most importantly, to *want* to learn. After all, we owe it to ourselves to ensure that our learning becomes a continuous process, particularly in a world that constantly changes.

1. Prepare before the session begins. Plan for both the physical space and the topic of the discussion.

- Agree to a time and private place for the session that will make you comfortable.

- Consider the issue beforehand. What is your perspective? Gather your own data to present. Think about how will you respond.

- Decide what you want to learn from the feedback.

Tip: Remember: you always have the right to check out feedback you've received with other sources of information. This can help validate the message.

What Would YOU Do?

Too Darn Hot

MAGGIE WAS DELIGHTED TO SPEND her summer vacation with her brother Tim at the beach. They talked about her new job, which was going great except for one thing. Maggie complained that when she talked to people about her work, she felt as if they were holding back on her. There didn't seem to be much of a dialogue. Tim speculated, with a twinkle in his eye, that maybe people were trying to tell her things that she didn't want to hear. After all, he went on, she was always pretty thin-skinned, always got upset if anyone ever tried to criticize her. Maggie snapped at him, hurt and angry. How dare he say that! Tim laughed and pointed out that she was doing it again. Tim was probably the only person in the world who could have said this to her without seriously jeopardizing their relationship. Something about the water and the sun made her more reflective than usual. He might have a point. Was her inability to accept criticism preventing people from telling her important things? Was it possible for her to become less defensive?

Steps for Receiving Feedback in a Formal Session

1. Prepare before the session begins.
2. Stay open to the feedback given.
3. Present your response carefully and rationally.
4. Decide what you can learn from the feedback.
5. Work with the feedback giver to develop an action plan for change.
6. Ask the feedback giver for support in following the action plan.

2. Stay open to the feedback given. This may be easier said than done, but unless you can lower your defensive shield and hear the feedback, the session will be a waste of time.

- If you suspect you might get upset, plan ahead for calming strategies (for example, breathing deeply, taking a short break, etc.).

- Listen carefully and try to understand the other person's point of view. Ask questions if you are unclear about any aspect of the feedback.

- Resist the urge to justify your behavior. Wait until your chance to respond and present your perspective clearly.

3. Present your response carefully and rationally. Remember that the process of giving and receiving feedback is a dialogue between two (or more) people. In a productive session, both participants will learn something. Your response will add information that the giver may not know and offer more to the shared understanding of the issue as well as broadening the possibilities for change.

4. Decide what you can learn from the feedback. As you and the feedback giver work through to a shared understanding of the issue, decide what you can learn from the feedback. After all, the primary purpose of the feedback is to help you grow professionally (and personally). If you are changing and growing, the organization will benefit from these changes too.

- Think about the validity of the feedback and requests for change.

- Consider the feedback giver's intention. What does he want from this session?

- Does this person have knowledge about the situation?

- What is your relationship to the feedback giver? Is he your supervisor, colleague, client? How does this relationship affect your response to the feedback?

- What facts can you agree on? Is there an area of disagreement that can't be resolved?

- Does the person want to work with you to help you improve?

- How can you improve in the future?

Feedback Readiness Checklist

Use this checklist to verify that you are ready to receive feedback.

Question	Yes	No
1. Did you help pick the setting?	✓	
2. Do you have preliminary information about the issue so you can be prepared?	✓	
3. Are you ready to listen and be open to the feedback?	✓	
4. Can you accept that you may have made a mistake or failed in some way?	✓	
5. Do you know how you will calm yourself or deal with the situation if you become upset?		✓
6. Can you identify what you hope to learn from the feedback?	✓	
7. Can you anticipate how you might change your behavior as a result of the feedback?	✓	

5. Work with the feedback giver to develop an action plan for change. If you don't participate in developing the action plan, you may not feel that it belongs to you. Commit only to what you know you can do.

6. Ask the feedback giver for support in following the action plan. Don't expect to be given an action plan and then be forgotten. Ask the feedback giver for help in following through. Suggest a time frame for achieving mini-goals, for example. And be sure to thank the other person for the feedback—it is a kind of gift for you.

Planning Commitment Worksheet

Use this tool after you have agreed to feedback you received and are planning your commitment. Share this commitment worksheet with the giver of the feedback to develop your formal action plan.

Describe your commitment.

I will not be rude to a customer calling for help.

What is the time frame?

As long as I am a helpdesk provider.

How will you achieve this?

When we have problems and everyone, including the helpdesk team and the customers, is tired and frustrated, I will speak slowly, listen carefully, take deep breaths, and always be polite.

How will this commitment help you obtain your goal?

I want to be an excellent helpdesk provider; I want to help customers solve their computer connection problems; and I want to be considered for advancement in the organization. To achieve these goals, I will strive to always help the customers solve their computer connectivity problems.

What might interfere with your meeting this commitment?

My temper. I am learning how to control my feelings of frustration and anger.

What support and resources do you need?

I need support from my team and the extra backup team that our supervisor promised to provide for us.

How sure are you that you can follow through on this commitment? Rate (1–10, 10 is absolutely sure).

I think I can overcome this problem. I've only lost my temper a few times in the past, and now, with support, I should be able to manage to behave politely on every call. Rating: 8

What You COULD Do.

Remember Maggie's dilemma?

Here's what the mentor suggests:

Maggie may suffer, like many of us, from living in a world in which her self-image is based mostly on her own assessment of her intentions. She tries to do her best; she works hard; she has the best of intentions. Therefore, she considers herself a good person and finds it hard to deal with criticism from others. However, while we blissfully judge ourselves by our own good intentions, we can become blind to the differences between our own intentions and the impact our behavior has on others, and this blindness often leads us to feel defensive in the face of critical feedback. "My intentions are only for the best—how can she criticize me?"

Feedback becomes a powerful tool for learning and self-awareness when we recognize that others perceive us differently than we do ourselves. If we can think of feedback as a way to learn about the mismatches between what we intend and the actual consequences of our actions on others, then we may come to see feedback as a gift, not an attack. It is possible for Maggie to become less defensive by becoming more curious and inviting dialogue. For example, she might want to listen closely when she is "talking to people about her work" to notice how much she is telling and how much she is asking her coworkers for their perceptions. If she tries asking others what they think and listening with a spirit of learning to what they say, even if it seems critical to her, she would probably experience much more open dialogue with her colleagues.

How to Manage
Feedback Problems

Feedback is not always easy to give or receive. The giver and receiver both need to be open—open to the fundamental benefits of the feedback and open to the possibility that the feedback being given may be based on incorrect assumptions. When both parties believe that the feedback can have real value, both can focus on the message and not rush through it. But before this point is reached, each may have to work through negative attitudes or associations.

You may find it difficult to give feedback because you

- believe that feedback is negative and unhelpful
- worry that the other person will not like you
- believe that the other person cannot handle the feedback
- have had previous experiences in which the receiver didn't change or was hostile to feedback
- feel the feedback isn't worth the risk

You may avoid receiving corrective feedback because you

- have the urge to rationalize and put up defenses against expected criticism
- believe that your self-worth is diminished by suggestions for improvement
- have had previous experiences in which feedback was unhelpful or unjustified

You may even find receiving affirming feedback uncomfortable because you

- don't want to be set apart from others
- feel others will be envious

Naturally, because feedback is based on interactions between at least two people, there are many moments when productive and honest communication could break down. The concerns listed above are normal but easily countered, because feedback is not only worth the risk of straining relationships, it is essential for the health of the organization.

Tip: Praise in public; criticize in private.

Some special situations, however, can pose problems beyond the norm. Personal relationships may interfere with discussing issues openly or directly. For example,

- Giving corrective feedback upward can become awkward or even professionally risky for you.
- Dealing with uncommunicative people can undermine the feedback process.
- Trying to give feedback during an emotionally charged situation can create real damage to relationships.
- Giving inappropriate feedback can cause more harm than good.

What Would YOU Do?

From This Moment On

9:54 A.M. That's what the clock on the computer screen read when Laura saw Betsy pass by her office, waving "hi." Almost an hour late. And she had just missed an important team meeting. That did it. Laura resolved to handle the situation before it got completely out of control. She sent Betsy an e-mail asking her to come to her office at 11:00. And then she took a deep breath. Ever since Laura and Betsy had become friendly, Betsy's work had started slipping. Now Betsy came in late frequently. Left early. And, last week, she did not turn in her weekly report. Laura felt she was being manipulated, and that annoyed her. Everyone else had surely noticed Betsy's slacking off. It was 10:05. Laura had less than an hour to figure out how she would handle this uncomfortable situation.

Think carefully about giving upward corrective feedback

Remember that receiving corrective feedback is difficult enough for many people, but to receive it from someone below you in the ranks may seem completely unacceptable.

You and other members of your team observe that your manager is inconsistent when reviewing and critiquing the team's work. As a result, some team members have become anxious about perfecting trivial matters and fall behind on the important project tasks. You discuss the problem with team members and decide that you need to raise the issue with your manager. How do you tell your supervisor that she is making a managerial mistake?

1. Decide whether the matter is worth taking action. If the impact of the supervisor's behavior can be corrected within the team, for example, then you may not want to approach your supervisor. Use the *Giving Feedback Upward* tool on the page 44 to help you make this initial decision.

Steps to Facilitate Giving Corrective Feedback Upward

1. Decide whether the matter is worth taking action.
2. Prepare carefully.
3. Make an appointment for a feedback session.
4. Describe the behavior and its impact on the team.
5. Pay close attention to your supervisor's response.
6. Make a suggestion or request.
7. Check for agreement or commitment for change.

2. Prepare carefully. In this case, you need to prepare very carefully. Plan how you will state the problem. Collect the data with notes, memos, job descriptions, events, dates, behavior, responses, results, etc.

3. Make an appointment for a feedback session. Don't surprise your manager! Let her know that you want to discuss an important issue with her privately. Ask for a particular time and place to meet.

4. Describe the behavior and its impact on the team. Depending on personalities and situations, you may want to begin in a friendly, upbeat manner. However, when you present the feedback, do so directly, simply, and accurately. Describe the behavior, not the personality. Avoid an accusatory tone of voice.

You could start by saying, "I'd like to discuss how we can prioritize tasks for project X."

Be sure to specify the effect of the manager's inconsistent behavior on the team's productivity.

You could say, "Matt and Heather are so focused on the formatting details, they aren't producing the content we need."

---

5. Pay close attention to your supervisor's response. Watch her body language. Is she becoming tense? Sitting back from you? Crossing her arms? These are signs of alienation. If she is leaning toward you, listening carefully, nodding her head, then she's trying to understand the issue—a more positive sign!

The verbal response you receive is, of course, the most important indicator of whether your boss understands the issue and is open to the feedback and to change. You can encourage and direct her response by asking periodically, "Does this make sense?"

6. Make a suggestion or request. Unless things are going badly, move from a statement of the problem to a possible resolution. You will know whether your manager is ready to meet this challenge or not. If so, she may join you in considering various options for improving the situation.

7. Check for agreement or commitment to change. Even if the process seems to have gone well, make sure that you are both clear about the commitment. Before the session concludes, ask something like, "So we agree that all of us will focus on the top priorities?" Try to have your manager answer with a simple, "Yes."

Finally, keep a record of the meeting, including the results.

Decide when feedback no longer works

In some cases, you'll find that a direct report just doesn't change. You go through several feedback sessions, agree to action plans, establish clear markers for success, but the person keeps behaving in the same problematic manner. There may be many possible reasons for this lack of progress—the employee just doesn't care, doesn't understand the necessity for change, disagrees with your management style, and so on. After a while, however, you, your

Giving Feedback Upward: Is It Worth It?

Use this tool to determine if the payoff of giving feedback upwards is worth the risk.

What is the problem?

Our supervisor is inconsistent when giving feedback to members of our team.

What could reasonable intentions be for the other person's actions?

Our supervisor may see differences in the work we do that we don't see.

How does it impact you?

Our supervisor's behavior discourages the team members who don't receive positive feedback when they have worked very hard and done an excellent job. In the long term, the quality of work could suffer, and some skilled employees might leave the group or even the organization.

Will this problem resolve itself or do you need to intervene?

I do not believe the problem will resolve itself. Unless one of us talks with her, our supervisor won't know there is a problem.

How open is this person to your feedback?

She says she is open to feedback and new ideas, but she doesn't always listen to us.

What are the possible negative consequences to giving feedback?

She may become angry with me for criticizing her management behavior. She may punish me in some way.

If the problem is resolved, how will your job and others' be easier?

If she does listen to the feedback, our supervisor could change her behavior to be fair and honest about her feedback to us. Or she could explain to us why she seems inconsistent to us, but has good reasons for what she does. If we understand her behavior as reasonable, we would feel better about our supervisor and our own work.

If the problem is not resolved, what will the consequences be?

Several team members will look for another position.

Are the payoffs worth the risks?

Yes, I believe the possibility for changing our supervisor's behavior is worth the risk. The team would work together more effectively.

---

team, and your organization do not need to suffer because of this employee's behavior (or lack of it). What to do? Prepare the path for the employee to move on.

- Consider one more time if there is anything you might be doing to add to the problem.

- Contact human resources and get their advice and help—for the employee and for yourself.

- Try another feedback session, but include another person in the room as a witness, perhaps an HR representative.

- Start documenting carefully what and how the employee says, agrees to, behaves, and misbehaves.

- Know that you are doing the best thing for everyone involved.

Tip: When dealing with vague or uncommunicative people, don't let your own frustration show.

Be patient when working with a noncommunicator

When you are dealing with quiet, shy, or uncommunicative people, slow the process down. Speak slowly yourself. Take long pauses.

Most importantly, ask open-ended questions—questions that require a response—such as "What was your rationale for telling the customer we couldn't help him?" or "How did you prepare for the presentation?" Not only do these types of questions need responses other than "yes" or "no," they show the person that you want to know more from his point of view; you are not just imposing your version of the problem.

Handle volatile situations with care

If the people involved are upset or angry, try to wait until they calm down before you engage in any feedback sessions.

Even when the surface emotions seem smooth, unsettled feelings can always bubble up again. So be prepared:

- Plan and rehearse how you will respond to excited outbursts. Try to refocus the person away from the point of dissension.

- Write down your feedback points so that you won't get distracted and forget them during the session.

- Remain composed yourself. Speak slowly and clearly.

- Avoid any comments that might be misconstrued as judgmental.

- Work on building small agreements about basic details, what happened, when, etc.

- Keep your feedback simple—limit the points to one or two per session.

Avoid giving inappropriate feedback

A common human reaction to seemingly unpleasant situations is to avoid them. This is often the case when face-to-face feedback is called for, but a manager uncomfortable with the feedback process or unwilling to invest the time needed for feedback adopts a different and less effective approach.

One of the helpdesk providers for a computer networking company is overwhelmed by the volume of calls from customers irate over a lapse in service. Even though Gonzalo has no power to solve the problem, his responses to the customers have been as reassuring and helpful as possible. Frustrated that the repair team can't seem to fix the problem, Gonzalo finally snaps at one particularly angry caller.

The caller asks for a manager and makes a formal complaint about the rude response she received from the helpdesk. The manager in turn sends an e-mail out to the entire helpdesk team, stating, "It has come to my attention that there have been instances of helpdesk providers being rude to our customers. This unprofessional behavior impacts your team, our customers, and our organization and will not be tolerated. This behavior does not apply to many of you, but we cannot let a few bad apples ruin our reputation and the future of our company. Every one of you must behave in a professional, respectful manner when dealing with our customers."

The manager in this case gave his team the feedback message: Unprofessional responses to customers will not be tolerated. However, he has not solved the problem. Rather, he has

- upset the entire team because no one is quite sure who the guilty people are

- heightened the level of anxiety of an already exhausted team

- protected himself behind the impersonal medium of e-mail

- not offered any models for "professional, respectful" behavior

- failed to support his team

- failed to find out what the problem really is

- failed to solve the problem

A more effective approach might follow this pattern:

Edward: Gonzalo, thanks for meeting with me.

Gonzalo: Sure. Is there a problem?

Edward: Yes and no. You're an excellent helpdesk provider—one of the most knowledgeable and tactful.

Gonzalo: Thanks, but then what's the problem?

Edward: Well, I'm trying to figure that out. Let me give you the facts. Yesterday, I received a phone call from a customer. She was upset about a response she received during a helpdesk call.

She said that the young man was rude to her and didn't help at all. I asked her to recall the exact conversation. What I heard was that the helpdesk professional explained that the service was down, and that he couldn't give a precise time for a restart of service. The customer demanded more information, and the young man shouted that he couldn't give her any more information.

Gonzalo: Hmm, that sounds like me, I'm afraid.

Edward: Yes, we traced the call to you. I know that behavior is not like you, so I'd like to hear your side of the story.

Gonzalo: I was rude to her. I don't deny it. We were all exhausted last night, and we couldn't do anything to solve the problem. It was frustrating, and I'm afraid I lost my cool when she started screeching.

Edward: Screeching?

Gonzalo: Ummm, shouting, anyway. It sounded like a screech to me.

Edward: Of course, you know we have to be polite to our customers, even when they are difficult.

Gonzalo: Yes, I know. I apologize. What can I do about it now?

Edward: Yes, what can we do about it now? What might help the situation? You say you were tired. Do we need more people on the helpdesk?

Gonzalo: Not usually, but when there's a problem like the server going down, then yes, we really need more help ourselves.

Edward: This sounds like a scheduling issue. We could have a backup team ready to jump in during emergencies. What do you think?

Gonzalo: That would be great! Thank you!

In this case, the manager took the time to:

- get the facts
- find out who was responsible for the problem (rather than accusing the entire team)
- talk face-to-face with the employee
- discover the deeper problem
- offer a realistic solution
- gain the gratitude, trust, and loyalty of his employee

This is a model of an effective feedback session.

What You COULD Do.

Remember Laura's dilemma?

Here's what the mentor suggests:

Laura has gathered some objective data about Betsy—arriving to work late, missing a meeting, failing to turn in an important report. But she has also jumped to some conclusions about the reasons for the behavior by attributing it to her becoming friendly with Betsy. She has decided that Betsy is using the friendship to manipulate her. Laura is starting to take action based on an emotional prejudgment. In short, Laura may be about to give feedback from very high on her ladder of inference, a dangerous perch from which to leap into a feedback conversation.

Laura needs to notice the assumptions and conclusions she has drawn about the reasons for Betsy's behavior and set them aside before she meets with Betsy. She should plan to tell Betsy the specific behavior she has noticed—coming in late, leaving early, missing the meeting, etc.—and to describe to Betsy the impact that behavior has had on the team. Then she needs to ask Betsy for her perspective on what is happening and why it is happening and be willing to listen to what Betsy has to say. For all Laura really knows, Betsy may suffer from some lack of awareness, or she may be having some serious personal problems that are affecting her work. If Laura approaches the feedback conversation with the firm belief that Betsy is taking advantage of her friendship or manipulating her (that is, from the perspective of her assumptions and judgments rather than from the objective data), it is unlikely that the feedback will be productive for either of them. Betsy's biased feedback will probably sound more like an attack, fail to resolve the problem, and damage their friendship as well!

Tips and Tools

Tools for
Giving Feedback

Planning a Feedback Session

Use this tool to organize before giving feedback during a scheduled session.

Name the issue or behavior that needs to be corrected or reinforced.

What is the impact of the issue or behavior on the team, in the department, or on the project?

What details do you have to describe the behavior accurately? (who, what, when)

What is the specific purpose of the feedback?

Describe possible barriers to giving this feedback. What can you do to overcome them?

What results do you want to produce? In the short run? In the long term?

Evaluating the Feedback Process

Use this chart after you have given feedback to determine what part of the process,
relationship, and results worked and what areas could be changed or improved.

Topic	What worked?	What could be changed or improved?
Process		
Planning for the meeting		
Setting the beginning of the meeting up for success		
Having a clear and logical process		
Developing a realistic action plan		
Relationship		
Communication style		
Reaction to the feedback		
Level of trust		
Level of mutual respect and learning		
Results		
Impact of changes		
Timeliness of changes		
Expectations met		

Feedback Readiness Checklist

Use this checklist to verify that you are ready to receive feedback.

Question	Yes	No
1. Did you help pick the setting?		
2. Do you have preliminary information about the issue so you can be prepared?		
3. Are you ready to listen and be open to the feedback?		
4. Can you accept that you may have made a mistake or failed in some way?		
5. Do you know how you will calm yourself or deal with the situation if you become upset?		
6. Can you identify what you hope to learn from the feedback?		
7. Can you anticipate how you might change your behavior as a result of the feedback?		

Planning Commitment Worksheet

Use this tool after you have agreed to feedback you received and are planning your commitment. Share this commitment worksheet with the giver of the feedback to develop your formal action plan.

Describe your commitment.

What is the time frame?

How will you achieve this?

How will this commitment help you obtain your goal?

What might interfere with your meeting this commitment?

What support and resources do you need?

How sure are you that you can follow through on this commitment? Rate (1–10, 10 is absolutely sure).

Giving Feedback Upward: Is It Worth It?

Use this tool to determine if the payoff of giving feedback upwards is worth the risk.

What is the problem?

What could reasonable intentions be for the other person's actions?

How does it impact you?

Will this problem resolve itself or do you need to intervene?

How open is this person to your feedback?

What are the possible negative consequences to giving feedback?

If the problem is resolved, how will your job and others' be easier?

If the problem is not resolved, what will the consequences be?

Are the payoffs worth the risks?

Test Yourself

Test Yourself offers ten multiple-choice questions to help you identify your baseline knowledge of how to give and receive feedback.

Answers to the questions are given at the end of the test.

1. Feedback has been described as the sharing of observations about job performance or work-related behaviors. Which of these best describes the recommended directions in which feedback can be productive?

a. Downward or laterally (with a colleague).

b. Downward to someone who reports to you.

c. Upward, downward, or laterally.

2. Doing your homework before a feedback session makes a difference in the success of the session. A key thing to keep in mind as you are planning is the receiver's perspective on the issue you'll be dealing with. What are potential sources of a crucial difference in perspective between the giver and the receiver?

a. Your intuition, which tells you the receiver is headed for trouble.

b. Race, gender, communication style, age.

c. Your personal involvement with the receiver.

3. We all recognize that there are times when giving feedback isn't advisable. Which of the following is a false statement?

a. DO NOT give feedback if either you or the receiver is too emotional to handle the process.

b. DO NOT give feedback if you're not prepared to receive feedback in return.

c. DO NOT give feedback if someone's actions or behavior have affected you personally and interfered with a good working relationship.

4. Feedback is not always easy to give or receive. Both the giver and the receiver need to be open to one particular possibility. Which of the following should both giver and receiver be ready to accept?

a. The feedback being given may be based on false assumptions.

b. The feedback session may damage your personal relationship.

c. Misguided actions based on faulty conclusions may result.

5. Often feedback calls for change in the giver or receiver. Experts have learned that some changes are easier to accomplish than others. Which of the following is the most difficult to change?

a. Job skills.

b. Personality characteristics.

c. Attitude.

6. Suppose the person to whom you are giving feedback is particularly shy and quiet. How might you best handle this situation?

   a. Ask open-ended questions that require a response.

   b. Work on making small agreements, one step at a time.

   c. Don't settle until you have all the details.

7. When you need to give feedback, should you give it as soon as possible or wait until you and the receiver have put some space between the event and the feedback session?

   a. Take time to do a thorough analysis of the situation.

   b. In general, give feedback as soon as you can after the event or behavior you want to encourage or correct.

8. Both feedback and performance evaluations focus on an employee's work and behavior. In what ways would a feedback session differ from a performance evaluation?

   a. One involves a face-to-face meeting; the other is a written review.

   b. One is looking at the past, and the other is looking toward the future.

   c. One is between two people; the other includes a whole team.

9. When planning on giving feedback upward, what is the first step you should take?

   a. Decide whether the payoff is worth the risk.

   b. Gather all the data and information you will need.

   c. Make an appointment ahead of time.

10. Which of the following are NOT consequences of giving inappropriate feedback?

  a. Failing to solve the problem.

  b. Raising the anxiety level of your direct reports.

  c. Retaining the status quo.

Answers to test questions

1, c. Feedback can be effectively given in different directions.

2, b. Be alert to ways in which gender, race, age, and communication style may lead to different perspectives on an issue.

3, c. It is important to give feedback when another person's actions or behavior have affected you personally.

4, a. There is always the possibility that the evidence on which the feedback is based may not be correct. One of the benefits of having a feedback session is that incorrect evidence or assumptions may be discovered and corrected.

5, b. Job skills are the easiest to change, and personality characteristics are the most difficult. Before you expect change in yourself or another person, make sure that the expectations reflect the nature of the change called for.

6, a. Asking open-ended questions makes it difficult for the other person to remain silent and distant.

7, b. Frequent feedback that is delivered during day-to-day working hours is more effective than infrequent feedback given at the end of an annual performance review.

8, b. During a performance evaluation, the supervisor reviews the employee's past work. During a feedback session, the emphasis is on the future and how the employee can grow.

9, a. Make sure the problem is severe enough and the potential change worth the risk of offending your boss.

10, c. Typically, inappropriate feedback makes a situation worse— not better, not even the same.

To Learn More

Notes and Articles

Harvard Business School Publishing. "Alternatives to the Annual Performance Review." *Harvard Management Update*, February 2000.

Companies can get rid of those troublesome yearly evaluations if they really want to. But it isn't an easy move to make. Managers have to change some fundamental assumptions about what really produces high performance. Companies have to work with employees differently on a variety of fronts, from feedback to compensation.

Harvard Business School Publishing. "Is There Any Good Way to Criticize Your Coworkers?" *Harvard Management Communication Letter*, March 2000.

Criticism is a part of all of our work lives. We see it as negative, painful, and uncomfortable both to give and to receive. But many experts believe that giving and receiving positive criticism can lead to continued growth. *Harvard Management Communication Letter* presents tips on when and how to criticize, and how to accept criticism from others.

Jamie Higgins and Diana Smith. "The Four Myths of Feedback." *Harvard Management Update*, June 1999.

The biggest obstacles to constructive feedback are some myths about feedback itself. Contrary to popular belief, defensiveness is okay; mistakes should not be covered up or punished. The whole point of feedback is to continually improve performance, and getting past the myths can help this happen.

Robert Kegan and Lisa Laskow Lahey. "The Real Reason People Won't Change." *Harvard Business Review* OnPoint Enhanced Edition. Boston: Harvard Business School Publishing, 2001.

Every manager is familiar with the employee who just won't change. Sometimes it's easy to see why—the employee fears a shift in power or the need to learn new skills. Other times, such resistance is far more puzzling. An employee has the skills and smarts to make a change with ease and is genuinely enthusiastic—yet, inexplicably, does nothing. What's going on? In this article, two organizational psychologists present a surprising conclusion. Resistance to change does not necessarily reflect opposition nor is it merely a result of inertia. Instead, even as they hold a sincere commitment to change, many people unwittingly apply productive energy toward a hidden competing commitment. The resulting internal conflict stalls the effort in what looks like resistance but is in fact a kind of personal immunity to change. An employee who's dragging his feet on a project, for example, may have an unrecognized competing commitment to avoid the even tougher assignment—one he fears he can't handle—that might follow if he delivers too successfully on the task at hand. Without an understanding of competing commitments, attempts to change employee behavior are virtually futile. The authors outline a process for helping employees uncover their competing commitments, identify and challenge the underlying assumptions driving these commitments, and begin to change their behavior so that, ultimately, they can accomplish their goals.

Maury A. Peiperl. "Getting 360-Degree Feedback Right." *Harvard Business Review*, January–February 2001.

Over the past decade, 360-degree feedback has revolutionized performance management. But one of its components—peer appraisal—consistently stymies executives and can exacerbate bureaucracy, heighten political tensions, and consume lots of time. For ten years, Maury Peiperl has studied 360-degree feedback and has asked: Under what circumstances does peer appraisal improve performance? Why does peer appraisal sometimes work well and sometimes fail? And how can executives make these programs less anxiety provoking for participants and more productive for organizations?

Edward Prewitt. "Should You Use 360-Degree Feedback for Performance Reviews?" *Harvard Management Update*, February 1999.

The use of 360-degree feedback—getting input on employee performance from peers and direct reports as well as managers and supervisors—has become widespread in developmental exercises such as team building and management preparation. But taking it one step further by tying 360-degree feedback to decisions such as salaries and promotions is much more controversial. On the one hand, most employees today work with many other people, and one manager may not be able to accurately assess their work. However, critics warn that using 360-degree feedback for appraisal goes against the human propensity to create hierarchies, protect status, and take revenge. Those who rate a boss or peer may feel uncomfortable about giving a frank evaluation. *Harvard Management Update* turned to practitioners and consultants for advice on making 360-degree feedback work in performance reviews. Includes a sidebar entitled "Using 360 for Performance Reviews? Tips for Success."

Books

Joe Folkman and Gene Dalton. *Turning Feedback into Change.* Provo, UT: Novations Group, 1996.

This book explores how to categorize, prioritize, and manage feedback you receive in your business and personal life. With attention to exploring when feedback is valuable, the book also addresses strategies for dealing with obstacles and achieving change.

Ferdinand F. Fournies. *Why Employees Don't Do What They're Supposed to Do and What to Do About It.* New York: Liberty Hall Press/McGraw-Hill, 1988.

This book discusses specific reasons why employees do not do what they are supposed to do and methods for addressing them. Each issue is explained with scenarios and a problem-and-solution format highlighting the major obstacles.

Harvard Business School Publishing. *Harvard Business Review on Managing People.* Harvard Business Review Paperback Series. Boston: Harvard Business School Press, 1999.

From managing diversity to exploring alternative workplaces to debunking myths about compensation, the topics covered in this collection of landmark articles from the *Harvard Business Review* address how to build organizations with judicious and effective systems for managing people.

Patti Hathaway. *Giving and Receiving Feedback: Building Constructive Communication.* Menlo Park, CA: Crisp Publications, 1998.

This is a self-study handbook with exercises, activities, and assessments. It covers how to receive critical feedback, how to cope with handling critical feedback, and how to give constructive feedback.

Karen Kirkland and Sam Manoogian. *Ongoing Feedback: How to Get it, How to Use It.* Greensboro, NC: Center for Creative Leadership, 1998.

This is a guidebook that provides specific advice on how to solicit feedback for professional and personal growth.

Karen Massetti Miller and Shirley Poertner. *The Art of Giving and Receiving Feedback.* West Des Moines, IA: American Media, 1996.

This book is in a self-study format and covers guidelines for effective feedback and tips on how to give and receive effective feedback.

eLearning Products

Harvard Business School Publishing. *Coaching for Results.* Boston: Harvard Business School Publishing, 2000. Online program.

Understand and practice how to effectively coach others by mastering the five core skills necessary for successful coaching:

- observing
- questioning
- listening
- feedback
- coming to agreement

Through interactive role play, expert guidance, and activities for immediate application at work, this program helps you coach successfully by preparing, discussing, and following up in any situation.

Harvard Business School Publishing. *Influencing and Motivating Others.* Boston: Harvard Business School Publishing, 2001. Online program.

Have you ever noticed how some people seem to have a natural ability to stir people to action? *Influencing and Motivating Others* provides actionable lessons on getting better results from direct reports (influencing performance), greater cooperation from your peers (lateral leadership), and stronger support from your own boss and senior management (persuasion). Managers will learn the secrets of "lateral leadership" (leading peers), negotiation and persuasion skills, and how to distinguish between effective and ineffective motivation methods. Through interactive cases, expert guidance, and activities for immediate application at work, this program helps managers to assess their ability to effectively persuade others, measure motivation skills, and enhance employee performance.

Sources for Giving Feedback

We would like to acknowledge the sources that aided in developing this topic.

Christopher Argyris, professor of education emeritus, Harvard Business School

Steve Armstrong, vice president, Kelly Services

Peter Baskette, manager, Genuity, Inc.

Anne Briggs, product director, Harvard Business School Publications

Richard Christiano, director of facilities administration and fulfillment, Harvard Business School Publishing

Jack Grossman and J. Robert Parkinson, authors, *Becoming a Successful Manager*

Jamie O. Harris, senior associate, Interaction Associates, Inc.

Jamie Higgins, senior consultant, Monitor Company

Jean-François Manzoni, associate professor of management, INSEAD

Hal Plotkin, writer and editor

Diana Smith, partner, Action Design

Notes

Notes

Notes

Notes

Notes

Notes

Notes

How to Order

Harvard Business School Press publications are available world-wide from your local bookseller or online retailer.

You can also call:
1-800-668-6780

Our product consultants are available to help you 8:00 a.m.–6:00 p.m., Monday–Friday, Eastern time. Outside the U.S. and Canada, call: 617-783-7450.

Please call about special discounts for quantities greater than ten.

You can order online at:
www.HBSPress.org